PRAGUE

AN ILLUSTRATED
GUIDE

An Illustrated guide

V RÁJI Book Shop,
Tomášská Street 10/23, Prague-1

◀ V RÁJI Book Shop and Gallery,
Maiselova Street 12/76, Prague-1

Concept, text and selection of photographs
© Marie Vitochová and Jindřich Kejř, 1998
Photography © Jiří Všetečka, 1998
Translation © David R. Beveridge, 1998
© V RÁJI Publishers, Prague 1998

ISBN 80-85894-62-9

V RÁJI Publishing House,
Maiselova Street 12/76, Prague-1

Jiří Všetečka
Marie Vitochová
Jindřich Kejř

AN ILLUSTRATED GUIDE TO
PRAGUE

V RÁJI
Publishing House
PRAGUE

St. Vitus Cathedral

S t. Vitus Cathedral is the main church of Bohemia. This gothic cathedral was founded by Charles IV in connection with the raising of the Prague Bishopric to the status of an Archbishopric in 1344. The cathedral's design is the work of the French master Matthieu d'Arras, who directed the construction until 1352, and the builder Peter Parler who succeeded him and completed the choir, the lower part of the main tower and the adjoining Golden Portal, the staircase, and the vaulted chancel. The eastern part of the cathedral was consecrated in 1385. After Parler, construction was taken over by his sons. The next stage in construction did not unfold until during the reign of the Jagellon dynasty. But the actual completion of the cathedral came only in the second half of the nineteenth century and the beginning of the twentieth century. Work was completed in 1929 under the direction of architects Josef Kranner, Josef Mocker, and Kamil Hilbert. The western neo-gothic facade consists of a pair of slender towers surrounding a high gable

The Cathedral Windows

The windows in St. Vitus Cathedral, made according to designs by important Czech painters and graphic artists, are outstanding. In artistic profile one in particular is striking: a window by Alfons Mucha, a celebration of Cyril and Methodius, St. Ludmila, St. Wenceslas (Václav), and the Slavic nations, in the Chapel of Provost Hora, also known as the New Archbishop's Chapel. This work of art attracts attention with its typical Art Nouveau coloring, even though this is a relatively late work of Mucha, from 1931. The drawings according to which Jan Veselý made the window are regarded as one of the most important examples of the artist's work in the period after the Slavic Epopeia. The window was ordered by the Slavie Bank.

In the Chapel of St. Sigismund, also called the Černín Chapel, the window at the right with figures of St. Luke, St. Joseph, St. Sigismund, St. Barnabas, and St. Mark was designed in 1870 by the painter Antonín Lhota

·S·LUKAS· ·S·IOSEPHUS· ·S·SIGISMVNDVS· ·S·GVILELMVS· ·S·BARNABAS· ·S·O

One of the most precious treasures of St. Vitus Cathedral is the St. Wenceslas (Václav) Chapel, from the period of construction of the cathedral by Matthieu d' Arras and Peter Parler, who completed this chapel in 1366. The chapel is dominated by an alabaster statue from 1373 of the patron saint of Bohemia, St. Wenceslas, probably the work of Henry Parler. During the renovation of the chapel in 1912–13, in which leading Czech artists, painters, sculptors, metal casters, and glass workers took part under the leadership of Kamil Hilbert, Franta Anýž restored the statue's polychromy and made a copper copy. From the St. Wenceslas Chapel, doors lead into the Crown Chamber, where the coronation jewels are deposited. In the center of the chapel is the Gothic tombstone of St. Wenceslas from the fourteenth century, modified by Kamil Hilbert, decorated with gilded plaster and with precious stones arranged in Art Nouveau style

The Wenceslas Chapel
The Coronation Jewels

The Coronation Jewels of the Czech kings are deposited in the Crown Chamber, which is entered from the St. Wenceslas Chapel. Opening the chamber requires the simultaneous presence of seven key custodians. The Royal Crown was dedicated to the main patron of the land, St. Wenceslas, and was probably made in 1345. The sceptre and the apple are from the first half of the sixteenth century. Also part of the St. Vitus treasure are the St. Wenceslas Sword and the Coronation Cross. The coronation robe with ermine, stole, belt, and maniple is deposited elsewhere. The Czech Coronation Jewels have not only great artistic and historical value, but above all moral value as a symbol of Czech statehood

The Interior of St. Vitus Cathedral

The vaulted chancel area is the original Gothic portion of the cathedral, built in 1344–85 by Matthieu d' Arras and Peter Parler. The great windows in the soaring choir are splendid. The three at the end, made in 1946–48, show the Holy Trinity with saints and donors according to a design by Max Švabinský. Above the arches of the arcades between the main nave and transepts runs the "triforium", above whose openings are busts of the family of Emperor Charles (Karel) IV and persons responsible for the building of the church. The triforium in the new part of the church features busts of those responsible for completing the construction of the cathedral centuries later

The Vladislav Hall
The Riding Stairs

The central room of the Old Royal Palace is the Vladislav Hall, two hundred feet long, fifty feet wide, and forty feet high. In its time this was the largest secular vaulted room in central Europe. It was built in the late fifteenth and early sixteenth centuries in the late Gothic style by Benedikt Ried of Pístov. The hall served for royal receptions. Councils met here, and banquets and even jousting tournaments were held. It even served as a market place. The hall continues today in its tradition as a site of important political and cultural events.

For jousting tournaments, knights rode up into the hall via the Riding Stairs. The staircase is arched over with a curved vault with truncated ribs

The Crucifix

During a tour of the St. Vitus Cathedral our attention is drawn by the great carved crucifix with the symbolic figure of the Virgin Mary beneath the cross, the work of sculptor František Bílek from 1896–98; it was installed on the wall of the north transept in 1927.
Bílek's emotional work is complemented by an upthrust arm with a candle-stick on the altar table

The Matthias Gate
The Spanish Hall

The gate to the first courtyard, called the Courtyard of Honor, by which one enters the castle from Hradčany Square (Hradčanské náměstí), is adorned with pillars and monumental statue groups of fighting titans, the work of sculptor Ignác František Platzer from 1770–71. Important visitors from all over the world are welcomed in the Courtyard of Honor. Ceremonies are held with the assistance of a unit of the Castle Guard, which also continuously guards all entrances to the castle.

The Matthias Gate, (Matyášova brána) built at the beginning of the seventeenth century and named after the current Emperor Matthias, forms a passage through the west palace wing of the Prague Castle

The Spanish Hall, in the north wing of the second court-yard, is one of the most important showplaces of the Prague Castle, the site of frequent political and cultural gatherings. The hall was built at the beginning of the seventeenth century according to a design by Giovanni Maria Filippi. The original decoration has not been preserved. The hall as it appears today is the result of several later modifications. The plaster decoration of the ceiling was created in 1754, during a re-modelling by Niccolo Pacassi. In 1774 the hall was ornamented with frescos, which however were covered in 1836 with a series of mirrors. The last modifications of the hall were made in the 1860s for the planned, though not realized, coronation of Emperor Franz Joseph as King of Bohemia. During the day the room is illuminated by a series of north windows; artificial lighting is provided by gilded chandeliers and wall lamps

St. George Basilica

L ocated on St. George Square with its Benedictine Convent in the Prague Castle, St. George Basilica originated sometime around the year 920 during the reign of Prince Vratislav I. In 973 the church was expanded and the convent founded. Further important construction was executed after the fire of 1142: at this time the church was elongated and received essentially its modern form. The white Romanesque towers are an indelible part of the panorama of the castle.

Today's appearance of the church's facade is Baroque. Among the most valuable parts of the basilica is the Chapel of St. Ludmila with wall murals from the end of the sixteenth century. St. Ludmila is painted on a triumphal arch, and her gravestone stands in the center of the chapel behind a marble rail with a metal grille. By the south transept is the chapel of St. Jan Nepomuk, whose apotheosis was created on the vault of the dome by the Czech Baroque master Václav Vavřinec Reiner

The Golden Lane

The most popular and most often visited part of the Prague Castle is the Golden Lane (Zlatá ulička) with its small, narrow, mostly two-floor houses, built against the ramparts during the time of the Jagellon Dynasty. They housed the castle archers as well as goldsmiths and, according to legend, perhaps also alchemists. The house at No. 22 deserves visitors' special attention: here for a time lived the writer Franz Kafka

The Royal Summer Palace

The Renaissance Royal Summer Palace, often called Belvedere or Queen Ann's Summer Palace, from the reign of Ferdinand I of Habsburg, is considered the most beautiful summer palace north of the Alps. Its model was designed by the Italian builder Paolo della Stella. The structure is characterized by an originally-conceived roof which is used effectively in views of the Prague Castle, and a fragile, airy, arcade-style gallery. In front of the Summer Chateau is the "Singing Fountain", named for the sound of water drops falling on bell metal. It was cast by the Tomáš Jaroš according to a design by Francesco Terzio. From the summer palace there is a gorgeous view of the northern, medieval part of the Prague Castle.

The Royal Gardens stretch from the street U Prašného mostu (At the Powder Bridge), along which one approaches the castle from the north, all the way to the Royal Summer Palace. They were laid out for Ferdinand I in 1534 by the architect Giovanni Spazio and landscape designer Francesco. The gardens were cared for also by Archduke Ferdinand of Tyrol and Emperor Rudolf II. Of the garden buildings and gazebos, the best known is the Great Ball Game Hall. The beautiful setting of the Royal Gardens invites one to peaceful walks, during which one can admire the Castle, St. Vitus Cathedral, and the Stag Moat

Gardens Around the Prague Castle

The Prague Castle is surrounded by gardens, from which one has gorgeous views of the city, the Castle, and the Cathedral. On the north side, beyond the Stag Moat, lies the most important of them, the Royal Gardens, with the Royal Summer Palace and the Singing Fountain. From here there is a view of the late gothic ramparts of the Castle. From the southern gardens beneath the castle, we may admire the Lesser Side and the panorama of the city on the Vltava. All the castle gardens are beautifully laid out and offer the visitor a wealth of aesthetic pleasures

The Archbishop's Palace

From Hradčany Square (Hradčanské náměstí) there is a fine view of the western part of the Prague Castle with St. Vitus Cathedral. The Archbishop's Palace, in the lower portion of the square in front of the Castle's Courtyard of Honor, is the seat of the Archbishop of Prague. The present form of the palace, the result of reconstruction in the 1760s, is the work of architect Jan Josef Wirch. In the center of the Rococo facade, richly adorned with stucco decorations, is the great coat of arms of Archbishop Antonín Příchovský. The palace's main portal has remained from the reconstruction according to a plan by Jean-Baptiste Mathey in 1675–79. Hidden behind the Archbishop's Palace lies the Sternberg Palace, which houses some collections of the National Gallery and where exhibitions of artistic works are held. The silhouette of the Archbishop's Palace is used in Prague panoramas along with the Castle

Hradčany Square

Hradčany Square (Hradčanské náměstí) stretches out in front of the west entrance to the Prague Castle. Evidently there was a market place on this site already in the tenth century. The original parish church of St. Benedict on the upper part of the square acquired its Baroque appearance around 1720. After the great Hradčany fire of 1541, new buildings and aristocratic palaces sprang up around the square. One of the largest is the Schwarzenberg Palace, which is a representative specimen of Renaissance palace architecture. Today it houses the exhibit of the Military Historical Museum with its collection of military memorabilia from earlier times. Hradčany Square is illuminated by original lanterns caste in 1865 in the Komárov iron works and placed in operation on 16 September 1867 by the Prague Municipal Gas Works

The Town Hall Steps
Loreto Street

Via the Town Hall Steps (Radnické schody) one can climb from Neruda Street (Nerudova ulice) on the Lesser Side (Malá Strana) to the place where Loreto Street (Loretánská ulice) empties onto Hradčany Square between St. Benedict's Church and the Toscana Palace. From the Town Hall Steps a pedestrian sees a magnificent spectacle looking upward, to where the south facade of the Schwarzenberg Palace looms up with its sgraffiato decorations. The sight evokes the atmosphere of Italian Renaissance cities. At the foot of the steps another route leads up to the right, to the Castle terrace, from which there are beautiful views over the roofs of the Lesser Side and the rest of Prague across the Vltava

F rom Loreto Square (Loretánské náměstí) via Loreto Street there is a view through toward Hradčany Square and St. Vitus Cathedral. On the lower part of the street, above the Town Hall Steps, stands the former Hradčany Town Hall (Hradčanská radnice), built at the beginning of the seventeenth century after Hradčany was raised to the status of a Royal Town in 1598. The sgraffiato facade with its remnant of the Imperial symbol has survived from this time, along with the symbol of the town of Hradčany on the portal.

Loreto Street is lined with showy palaces: the Hrzán Palace (No. 177/9), the Martinic Palace (No. 181/4), the Trauttmansdorff Palace (No. 180/6), and the Toscana Palace (No. 182/5)

The Loreto

On the eastern part of Loreto Square lies the complex of the Prague Loreto with its Church of the Nativity, built in 1735–37 by Kilián Ignác Dienzenhofer. The design of the interior and the lengthening of the nave are usually attributed to Jan Jiří Aichbauer. Among the ceiling paintings in the church's chancel, outstanding is the work of Václav Vavřinec Reiner, The Sacrifice of Christ, and on the main altar the painting of The Birth of the Lord by Jan Jiří Heinsch. The facade of the Loreto was also built by Kilián Ignác Dienzenhofer, in 1720–23, but according to a design by his father, Kryštof Dienzenhofer. In the front tower from 1693 are located the well-known Marian Bells.

Inside the complex stands a copy of the Holy House in Loreto, Italy, built here in 1626–27 by Giovanni Battista Orsi at the instigation and expense of Benigna Kateřina of Lobkovice. Around the little house run ambits containing a total of seven chapels. Worthy of note is the Loreto Treasury, found in the second floor of the facade wing of the Loreto. The most famous item in the collection is the Diamond Monstrance

The New World

T he "New World" (Nový Svět) lies to the north of Loreto Square, behind the Capuchin Monastery. In the Middle Ages it formed a sort of suburb to Hradčany. This whole section, through which lead the streets Černín, Capuchin (Kapucínská), and New World (Nový Svět), is unusually picturesque. The structures stem mostly from the eighteenth and early nineteenth centuries. Among the most interesting buildings are the houses "At the Golden Pear" (U Zlaté hrušky – No. 77/3) with its famous restaurant, "At the Golden Griffin" (U Zlatého Noha – No. 76/1) with a plaque com-memorating the stay of the astrono-mer Tycho de Brahe, and "At the Golden Plow" (U Zlatého pluhu – No. 90/25) with a reference to the violi-nist František Ondříček. In Černín Lane we find, over house No. 97/5, a statue of St. Jan Nepomuk from the middle of the eighteenth century

The Church of the Virgin Mary of the Angels

O n the lower part of Loreto Square lies the complex of the Capuchin Monastery with the Church of the Virgin Mary of the Angels. This simple little church was built at the beginning of the seventeenth century for the Capuchins, who came to Prague with their leader Lawrence of Brindisi, later made a saint. On land belonging to Markéta of Lobkovice they built a monastery, and they were supported in their religious fervor by the Catholic nobility. According to legend, their frequent ringing of the church bell bothered the astronomer Tycho de Brahe, who lived nearby, and therefore Emperor Rudolf II complained about the Capuchins. The single-nave Capuchin church is famous especially for its nativity scene with life-size figures. The view from the New World offers us the northern part of the Church of Mary of the Angels with the monastery, at left the Loreto, and the summit of Petřín with its observation tower

The Černín Palace

This view from Černín Lane in the New World is toward part of the north facade of the Černín Palace, which occupies the whole western side of Loreto Square. The Palace was built by Count Humprecht Jan Černín of Chudenice. His architect in the last third of the seventeenth century was Francesco Caratti. Work then continued in the first part of the eighteenth century under the architect František Maxmilian Kaňka, who also designed the palace garden, as well as Anselmo Lurago. Today this building, the largest Baroque palace in Prague, houses the Ministry of Foreign Affairs of the Czech Republic

The Strahov Monastery

A n indelible part of the Prague panorama is the complex of the Strahov Monastery with the abbot's Church of the Ascension of the Virgin Mary. This church, now Baroque, had its precursor already in a Romanesque basilica from the end of the twelfth century. In the church are deposited relics of St. Norbert, founder of the Premonstrate Order.

From the west, from Pohořelec, one enters the monastery through a Baroque gate built in 1742 by Anselmo Lurago, adorned with a statue of St. Norbert by Jan Antonín Quittainer. On the north side of the extensive Strahov courtyard stands the small Gothic-Renaissance church of St. Roch, built at the beginning of the seventeenth century according to

a design by architect Giovanni Maria Filippi at the expense of Emperor Rudolf II, as thanks for the retreat of the plague. From the terrace in front of the Strahov Monastery there is a beautiful view of the Prague Castle, the Lesser Side (Malá Strana), the city beyond the river, and to the right the summit of Petřín Hill with its observation tower and Church of St. Lawrence

The Strahov Library

One of the prides of the Strahov Monastery is the Strahov Library with its Theological Hall, built by Giovanni Domenico Orsi. The vault of the hall has its original early Baroque plaster decorations and paintings from the begining of the eighteenth century by František Kristian Nosecký. The extensive collection of theological literature includes remarkable illuminated manuscripts. The center of the hall is occupied by globes from the seventeenth and eighteenth centuries. The Philosophical Hall forms an independent building with a Classical facade from the end of the eighteenth century. It is decorated with a ceiling painting, The History of Mankind, by Franz Anton Maulbertsch, a painter of the Viennese Rococo. Among other things, one finds here a collection of Baroque book bindings and rare scientific printed materials

The Church of St. Lawrence on Petřín Hill

I f we set out along the Gothic wall of the ramparts from the time of Charles IV, called "The Hunger Wall", toward the Petřín Hill observation tower on the Lesser Side, we come to the Church of St. Lawrence (sv. Vavřinec), built according to a plan by Kilián Ignác Dienzenhofer and completed by Ignác Palliardi in 1770. The construction was financed by the Brotherhood of Prague Cooks. On the main altar is the painting The Torture of St. Lawrence. Beside the church is the Chapel of the Lord's Tomb. The Petřín Hill Observation Tower is a free imitation of the Eiffel Tower in Paris. It is two hundred feet high and was built in 1891 as part of the Jubilee Exhibition. Not far away is the Labyrinth, built as a miniature of the former south gate to Vyšehrad from the time of Charles IV; it contains an entertaining mirrored walkway, which leads the persistent to an illusory image picturing the battle of Praguers with the Swedes on the Charles Bridge in 1648. From Petřín Hill one can descend by the cable car to Újezd Street on the Lesser Side

The Palace of the Lords of Hradec

Dominating the whole lower part of the New Castle Steps (Nové zámecké schody), the Palace of the Lords of Hradec is one of the most beautiful Czech Renaissance palaces. One can't miss its especially striking facade gables, typical of the Czech Renaissance. Jáchym of Hradec had it built in 1562–64, and Adam of Hradec expanded it twenty years later. Starting in the beginning of the seventeenth century its owners were the Slavata family, and in the second half of the seventeenth century the palace was remodelled in Baroque style by Domenico Giovanni Orsi. The palace is connected with the Thun-Hohenstein Palace on Neruda Street (Nerudova ulice) and today belongs to the complex of the Italian Embassy

The Church of St. Nicholas

The Baroque architecture of the Church of St. Nicholas (chrám svatého Mikuláše) on the Lesser Side is uniquely impressive even among the imposing churches of Prague, and this church is one of the most valuable religious landmarks in all of central Europe. The church, to which is attached a former Jesuit college, stands on the upper part of Lesser Side Square (Malostranské náměstí). Both of the Dienzenhofers, father and son, shared in building this unique structure, in 1703–11 and 1737–52, along with Anselmo Lurago, who was responsible for the high bell tower (1750–56). In the nave of the church we may admire paintings and statues representative of the High Baroque. The ceiling fresco above the nave, celebrating St. Nicholas, is one of the largest in Europe, painted by Jan Lukáš Kracker. The fresco in the dome, devoted to the Holy Trinity, is by F. X. Balko. The four massive statues of the Church Teachers are by the sculptor Ignác František Platzer

The Church of the Virgin Mary under the Chain

The precursor to today's church (kostel Panny Marie pod Řetězem) at the end of Lázeňská Street (Spa Street) originated in the late twelfth century as a Romanesque three-nave structure. An extensive Gothic reconstruction began in the middle of the fourteenth century, but of the original plan all that were built were the two massive square Gothic towers and the chancel, which one enters via the courtyard behind the towers. Today's appearance of the unfinished church is Baroque, and the interior too is decorated with Baroque paintings and sculpture. Worthy of note above all is the main altar painting, depicting the Maltesian Knights adoring the Madonna during a battle with the Turks at Lepanto (Greece) in 1571, the work of Karel Škréta. The church was the center of a fortified compound of the Knights of the Order of St. John of Jerusalem, later the Maltesian Knights, which had its own self-administration, being exempted from the legal power of the Lesser Side government

The Church of the Virgin Mary of Victory

This church (kostel Panny Marie Vítězné) on Carmelite Street (Karmelitská ulice) beneath Petřín Hill was originally built by German Lutherans at the beginning of the seventeenth century. However, only a short time after the Battle on White Mountain (1620), after the victory of the Counter-Reformation, the church was acquired by the Carmelites, who later reconstructed it into today's Baroque form. The Carmelites among other things rotated the orientation of the church, which originally faced the Petřín Hill, so that the chancel and main altar are now on the western end. Beneath the church is a crypt with remains of Carmelites and benefactors of the order. The main treasure of the church is the famous wax figure of the Infant Jesus of Prague, which was brought from Spain and given to the Carmelites in 1628 by their patron Polyxena of Lobkovice

The Town Beneath the Prague Castle

The beginnings of settlement on the site of today's Lesser Side reach back to the ninth and tenth centuries, but not until 1257 did the Přemysl King Otakar II found an actual town here, summoning colonists and ordering it to be fortified with ramparts. Originally it was called New Town Under the Prague Castle, then starting in the fourteenth century the Lesser Town of Prague. Independent units surrounded by fortifications were the Palace of the Bishop of Prague with its garden, to the right of the bridge towers, and the compound of the Knights of St. John with its Church of Mary Under the Chain to the left. Today's image of the Lesser Side, however, was created mainly in the eighteenth century, for the Baroque period adorned the town with magnificent aristocratic palaces and gardens, and the victorious Catholic Church with glorious churches whose domes and towers project above the roofs of the noble seats. Tourists find the Lesser Side (Malá Strana), with its many valuable historical buildings and distinctive color, to be one of the most attractive parts of Prague

Waldstein Street

From the Malostranská (Lesser Side) metro station via Waldstein Street (Valdštejnská ulice), lined with palaces and their gardens, we reach shortly Waldstein Square (Valdštejnské náměstí) and then via Thomas Street (Tomášská ulice) we come to Lesser Side Square (Malostranské náměstí), the center of the Lesser Side. Along the left side we pass the extensive complex of the Waldstein Palace with its riding stables and garden, and on the right side the Fürstenberg Palace, today housing the Polish Embassy, the Kolovrat Palace (in the photo), and others – the Little Fürstenberg and Palffy Palaces. Behind the palaces on the right side, gardens exemplifying Baroque landscape architecture and today open to the public extend up the south-facing hill all the way to the Castle

The Waldstein Palace and Garden

Albrecht Wenzel Eusebius von Waldstein, Imperial Generalissimo and Duke of Friedland, had this monumental palace with garden, sala terrena adjacent to the palace, and the Waldstein Riding Stables built as his main Prague headquarters. This warrior and entrepreneur, for some a possible contender to the Bohemian throne, after 1620 one of the most powerful men of his time, had himself built in 1623–29 a splendid seat corresponding to his exceptional standing, working with the Italian architects Andrea Spezza, Nicolo Sebregondi, and Giovanni Pieroni. In the facade wing of the palace is the main hall with stuccoed vault and a ceiling painting of Albrecht von Waldstein as the god Mars. Scenes from the Trojan War adorn the ceiling of the sala terrena. The originals of the bronze statues from the garden from 1625–26 by the Dutch sculptor Adrian de Vries are today replaced by copies: the original statues were hauled off by the Swedish army as war booty and are now in Drottningholm. Today the Waldstein Palace houses the Senate of the Czech Parliament

Lesser Side Square

Already in the tenth century on the site of today's Lesser Side Square (Malostranské náměstí) there was a market place, which along with surrounding buildings constituted a settlement beneath the Prague Castle. The importance of this central space of the settlement grew when, during the reign of the Přemysl King Otakar II, the settlement was granted official status as a town. The Church of St. Nicholas and the Jesuit College associated therewith divided the square into an upper and lower part. The upper part of the square was called Italian Square (Vlašský rynk); the joint title of Lesser Side Square began to be used only after the middle of the nineteenth century. The square is surrounded by several palaces: among the most beautiful are the Sternberg Palace (No. 7/19), with a painting of the Virgin Mary and the Sternberg coat of arms on its facade (today belonging to Parliament) and the Kaiserstein Palace, famous above all for the fact that the world-famous opera singer Emma Destinnová lived here in 1908–14

The Romantic Lesser Side

The uniqueness of the Lesser Side consists not only in the magnificent palaces of the nobility and the pompous Baroque churches, but also in the maze of narrow streets and lanes lined with middle-class houses, which rise like a tide from the banks of the Vltava up toward the Prague Castle and along the slopes of Petřín Hill and Strahov. From above, from the Castle terrace or from the Strahov Monastery, they fuse into a wavy surface of red and brown roofs with white and pink chimneys, interwoven with the green of the Lesser Side gardens. Lesser Side nooks, lanes, courtyards, passages, and houses with their long-time residents create the town's special intimate atmosphere, where despite the streams of tourists time flows at its own tempo

Lesser Side
House Signs

When wandering along Lesser Side streets we notice frequent pictures, sculptures, and reliefs – house signs, closely associated with a house, its history, or the life and work of its owners. These decorations on house facades used to serve for identification of the house or its owner, for designation of the owner's professional trade, or as an expression of gratitude and hope for protection. For example the sign "At the Three Fiddles" (U Tří housliček) on Neruda Street refers to the Edlinger family of violin makers, in whose workshop originated outstanding instruments for three generations. According to legend one of their violins was played by Beethoven. The sign on the house "The Blue Fox" (Modrá liška) on the Kampa Island (Na Kampě) according to legend recalls a former game-keeper's lodge on this site

Lesser Side Parks

The quaintness of the Lesser Side is created in part by green gardens and public parks. The entrance to the well-known Vojan Park is from the street U Lužického semináře. This was once the garden of a Carmelite Convent. Today it is a public park named for the important Czech actor Eduard Vojan, who was born on nearby Míšeňská Street. From here one can catch sight of the towers of the Churches of St. Thomas, St. Joseph, and St. Nicholas on the Lesser Side, as well as the Prague Castle with its cathedral. Another popular place is the extensive park on Kampa Island by the Sova Mills (Sovovy mlýny). From the park there is a beautiful view of the river, its damns, the Charles Bridge, the Old Town bank, and the National Theater. The Lesser Side parks form oases amid the bustle of the city and offer visitors tranquility and rest

Čertovka
The Venice of Prague

The island of Kampa is separated from the Lesser Side by a canal called since the end of the nineteenth century Čertovka. From the part of the Charles Bridge before the Lesser Side Bridge Towers a view opens up toward the best known building in this part of the Lesser Side – the Velkopřevorský Mill, belonging originally to the compound of the Knights of St. John. To the delight of visitors, its mill wheel, driven by the water of Čertovka, still slowly turns. The waters of Čertovka are a paradise for water lovers in summer, while in winter they are a refuge for water birds. On the lower part of Čertovka, the walls of houses from the eighteenth and nineteenth centuries rise directly from the water – hence the name The Venice of Prague

The Old Castle Steps
The Lesser Side from the Petřín Hill

From Klárov on the Lesser Side (near the Malostranská metro station) one can take a shortcut to the Prague Castle via the Old Castle Steps (Staré zámecké schody), built in the mid-seventeenth century to replace an old road. To the right of these steps, which are celebrated in Czech songs, one can see zig-zagging upward the original route, which led from the ford across the Vltava toward the Castle. Above the steps, from the terrace in front of the gate in the Black Tower (Černá věž) one has a view down on the Lesser Side palace gardens, which climb all the way up to the buildings of the Castle, and the city on both banks of the river, and we can see upstream along the Vltava all the way to the other castle of Prague – Vyšehrad

An incomparable experience is the view from the Petřín Hill Observation Tower. This panorama includes part of the Lesser Side, dominated by the Church of St. Nicholas, with palaces and houses beneath the south ramparts of the Prague Castle leading downward all the way to the Vltava. Beyond the bend of the Vltava arches the splendid Art Nouveau Svatopluk Čech Bridge (Čechův most), which we reach from the Lesser Side by following along the embankment, and linking to it Paris Avenue (Pařížská třída), which empties into Old Town Square (Staroměstské náměstí). The extensive complex of buildings on the left side of the Vltava before the Svatopluk Čech Bridge are today the offices of the Premier of the Czech Republic

Bertramka

In the nearby district of Smíchov, on Mozart Street at No. 169/2, stands hidden among trees the well-known building called Bertramka, originally a farmstead from the second half of the seventeenth century, named after its former owner Bertram. During his visits to Prague Wolfgang Amadeus Mozart stayed here as guest of the owners of Bertramka at the time, the composer František Dušek and his wife Josefína, an outstanding Czech singer. At Bertramka Mozart completed his opera Don Giovanni, which received its world premiere at the Estates Theater in Prague. Bertramka is open to the public, and concerts and performances by leading Czech artists are held here

The Old Town Square
The Astronomical Clock and Calendar

S ince time immemorial Old Town Square (Staroměstské náměstí) has been the heart of the city. We have reports of a large market place on this site from as early as the eleventh century. A dominant position on the square is held by the complex of buildings of the Old Town Hall with its massive square tower, a symbol of the city's power and the wealth of its inhabitants. As a counterpoise to secular power, the twin towers of the Týn Church (Church of the Virgin Mary in Front of Týn), embracing its high facade, gaze onto the square from the other side. The bourgeois cathedral, as the Týn Church is also sometimes known, stood here already at the end of the twelfth century, in a somewhat more modest form. Old Town Square has remained to this day the natural center of the city, a place where even now important political and social-cultural events take place

T he famous astronomical clock on the Old Town Hall, made in 1410 by Mikuláš of Kadaň and improved in 1490 by Hanuš of Růže, with its late Gothic decoration, is the most admired attraction in Prague. Each hour, to visitors' delight, moving Apostles appear in the upper windows, and their walk is terminated by the bell of Death and the crowing of the cock. The clock consists of two parts. The upper part shows the revolution of the Sun and the Moon and the time of day; the calendar below shows the days and months of the year. The calendar, with pictures from the Czech countryside, was painted by Josef Mánes; the figures of the Apostles along with the sculptures on the lower part of the clock are the work of Vojtěch Sucharda

The Old Town Square in the Evening

The admiration of viewers for the Astronomical Clock is no less in the evening, and crowds of viewers look upward every hour. Most of the houses in the row on the south side of the square have a Romanesque or Gothic core. Today, however, with evening lighting, they form a remarkable backdrop to the venerable square with their predominantly Baroque and Classical facades. From this part of the square one can exit into the narrow Melantrich Street, named after the printer Jiří Melantrich of Aventinum, as commemorated by a plaque on the building "At the Two Cammels" (U dvou velbloudů) (No. 474). Via this street and on across the Havel Marketplace we can walk all the way to Wenceslas Square (Václavské náměstí)

The Old Town Hall

The residents of the Old Town finally gained permission from King Jan Lucemburský in 1338 to establish their own Town Hall. Immediately they purchased the first town hall building and began constructing the massive square tower, an expression of their power and wealth. Soon arose also the Town Hall Chapel with its beautiful Gothic oriel, which was consecrated in 1381 and is one of the outstanding examples of Gothic architecture from the time of Charles (Karel) IV. As the town's political and economic importance grew, the Town Hall too was expanded to include further buildings in the late Gothic and Renaissance style, finally achieving today's historical beauty. Not by chance, the Baroque left almost no traces here, for by the time of the Baroque remodellings the political power and independence of the city administration was only a legend. Today the Old Town Hall and its historical buildings again serve for democratic administration of the whole capital city. In their show-case halls the most distinguished visitors are received – recently the Queen of the United Kingdom of Great Britain and Northern Ireland, Elizabeth II, was a guest of Prague for the very first time

Little Square

L ittle Square (Malé náměstí), whose triangular shape has remained since Romanesque times, has retained its intimate character as well. One of the most showy buildings is No. 142/3, called "U Rotta" (Rott's House). This originally Romanesque building has been remodelled several times, but the cellar has remained in its original Romanesque and Gothic form. The building acquired its Neo-Renaissance appearance in 1896–97 during remodelling according to a design by the architect Eduard Rechziegel. The paintings of trades and agriculture are by Láďa Novák and Arnošt Hofbauer according to drawings by Mikoláš Aleš. In the middle of the square stands a splendid fountain with its original iron grille from the Renaissance

The House "At the Minute"

One of the most attractive buildings on Old Town Square is "At the Minute", which continues the row of buildings of the Town Hall. At its core a Gothic house, it was remodelled in late Gothic and Renaissance style, for the last time sometime before 1615. The arcade, through which one can pass to Little Square (Malé náměstí), was opened only after remodelling in 1939–40. In 1889–96 the writer Franz Kafka lived in this house with his parents. The facade of the building is ornamented with beautiful mannerist sgraffito on biblical and mythical subjects (the Battle of the Lapithae with the Centaurs), along with motives from contemporary Renaissance legends. The corner of the building is highlighted by a Classical statue of a lion holding a coat of arms in its front paws

The City of the Eucharist Chalice

In the time of the Hussite Revolution, the City of Prague stood at the head of Hussite Bohemia. In the Town Hall decisions were made on the future course of domestic and foreign policy and on defense against warring crusades, and negotiations were held with allies. During this period without a king, until the acsension of Jiří of Poděbrady to the Czech throne, the municipal government, i.e. the eighteen councillors, had unbelievable power in their hands, which was very unusual for the time. The city negotiated with Venice, for example (in 1420), sent out its missions to the courts of European rulers and to church councils, and even had born noblemen in its services. The city churches were filled with the pious people, who received communion in both kinds. The Týn Church saw its greatest glory in the period when the Hussite priest Jan Rokycana worked here, and then during the reign of Jiří of Poděbrady. The facade gable of the church was adorned with a eucharistic chalice and a statue of the "Hussite King" Jiří of Poděbrady, elected by the Czech Estates on 2 March 1458 in the Old Town Hall. A reminder of this glorious time in the nation's history is the massive Hus Monument on the square, a splendid example of Art Nouveau style by the sculptor Ladislav Šaloun, created for the 500th anniversary of the burning of Master Hus at the stake in Constance on 6 July 1415

Storch's House

Worthy of special attention on Old Town Square is Štorch's House, erected by the builder František Tichna in 1896–97 according to a design by Friedrich Ohmann on the site of a Gothic building, in the style of the fashionable "Vladislav Gothic" for the publisher Alexander Storch. The facade is covered by frescos and colorful sgraffito decorations according to a design by Mikoláš Aleš, along with plant motives that already anticipate Art Nouveau. At the top rises a graduated gable and at the level of the second floor above ground level there is a beautiful oriel with a turret-style roof of sheet metal, which is a reminder of the original Gothic building. The doors and windows in the most varied shapes were also inspired by the "Vladislav Gothic". The Madonna under the baldachin at the right over the entrance and the statues of apostles in the corners of the sculpturally decorated oriel form a sort of miniature counterpart to the decoration of the oriel in the Town Hall Chapel. The paintings on the facade show figures from history – Jan Amos Komenský, St. Wenceslas on his horse, a saint in a cloak, and a monk writing. Storch's emblem – a stork – is also here, along with symbols of the Kingdom of Bohemia and the City of Prague. The decorations are completed by "company insignia"

The Old Town Church of St. Nicholas

The Church of St. Nicholas (kostel sv. Mikuláše) in the Old Town (Staré Město) is mentioned for the first time in connection with a flood on the Vltava in 1273. In the original Gothic parish church the reformers Jan Milíč of Kroměříž and Matěj of Janov preached for a time. The designer of the Baroque church was Kilián Ignác Dienzenhofer. The south facade with its two towers and dome faced the original small "Poultry Market" between the buildings of the Town Hall and Little Square (Malé náměstí). In the interior of the church are valuable paintings in the dome on motives from the lives of St. Nicholas and St. Benedict and from the Old Testament by Cosmas Damian Asam, from 1735–36. The church has a colorful history. Among other things it was temporarily rented to the Russian Orthodox Church, and since 1920 it has served the Czechoslovak Hussite Church, which was proclaimed at this site in January of the same year. The congregation here can take credit for organizing frequent concerts in the premises of the church

The tower of Old Town Hall projects with dignity over the rooftops in the illuminated center of the age-old city, the towers and dome of St. Nicholas Church appearing as though pressed against it. The lighted twin towers at left belong to the Church of St. Havel, and the church nave rising to the heights beyond is the Church of the Virgin Mary of the Snows in the New Town. Via Paris Avenue (Pařížská třída), lined with imposing Art Nouveau buildings and conceived as an unusually broad street for its time, one can pass through from the banks of the Vltava directly to Old Town Square

The Church of St. Gall and the Gall Marketplace

One of the oldest churches in Prague, this church dedicated to St. Gall (Havel) has an interesting history. Even before the Gall quarter was established in the thirteenth century, a little Romanesque church stood here. Charles IV donated relics of St. Havel to the new Gothic church in 1353. In 1358 the reformers Konrad Waldhauser and Jan Milíč of Kroměříž preached here, then in 1404 Jan Hus and in 1412 Štěpán of Páleč. During the Hussite Revolution the church passed into the ownership of the reformers, and not until 1627 was it given to the Carmelites. After an early Baroque remodelling in the seventeenth century, at the beginning of the eighteenth century a fundamental Baroque reconstruction was undertaken according to a design by Pavel Ignác Bayer. The dynamically wavy facade is perhaps the result of collaboration with Jan Santini-Aichl. The main facade of the Church of St. Havel faces the Gall (Havel) Marketplace, surrounded by buildings whose cores are Romanesque-Gothic. Just as in the Middle Ages, today as well a lively bustle prevails in the marketplace

The Anežka Cloister

One of the oldest religious complexes in Bohemia is the Anežka Cloister (Anežský klášter) at Anežská ulice 811–814/12 in Prague's Old Town. The cloister was founded by King Wenceslas I (Václav I) at the instigation of his sister Anežka (Agnes) sometime after 1233. As recorded in the Chronicles, he had built "a monastery for the Mendicant Brothers in honor of St. Francis and a convent for nuns of the Order of St. Clare in honor of the Saviour." The first abbess of the cloister was Anežka, and after the model of St. Clare she abdicated her position after three years. This highly educated princess, who refused offers of advantageous dynastic marriages and gave preference to serving Christ, the poor, and the ill, was an important figure of the thirteenth century by virtue of her breadth of vision, her contacts, and her diplomatic abilities. In the eventful year of 1989 Anežka Česká (Agnes of Bohemia) was declared a saint.

Within the cloister complex are the Gothic churches of St. Francis and St. Salvator, and the cloister buildings placed according to Cistercian custom close to the banks of the Vltava. In the middle of the complex was laid out the cloister garden, serving members of the order as the only place for discussions. At the present time the cloister houses a permanent exhibit of paintings from the nineteenth century, and exhibitions and concerts are held here on a regular basis

The Carolinum

The Gothic oriel of the University Chapel of Saints Kosmas and Damián from the late fourteenth century is richly decorated with coats of arms, gargoyles, and turrets. The chapel adjoins a great hall, the traditional historical core of Charles University, where graduation ceremonies and academic festivities take place. The university was founded on 7 April 1348 by Charles IV as the first institution of higher education in central Europe. In the early fifteenth century important reformers like Jan Hus, Jeroným of Prague, Jakoubek of Stříbro, and Štěpán of Páleč worked at the university. In the time of Charles IV and his son Wenceslav IV, students were registered here from all over the Holy Roman Empire, and the university won acclaim for its free thinking. After 1620 the Counter-Reformation affected the university: soon it was placed under the administration of the Jesuits, merged with their college in the Clementinum, and titled the Charles-Ferdinand University. After 1918 the title Charles University was restored. The entrance to the age-old Carolinum is at No. 541/3 on the street Ovocný trh (Fruit Market) or from No. 9 on Železná ulice (Iron Street)

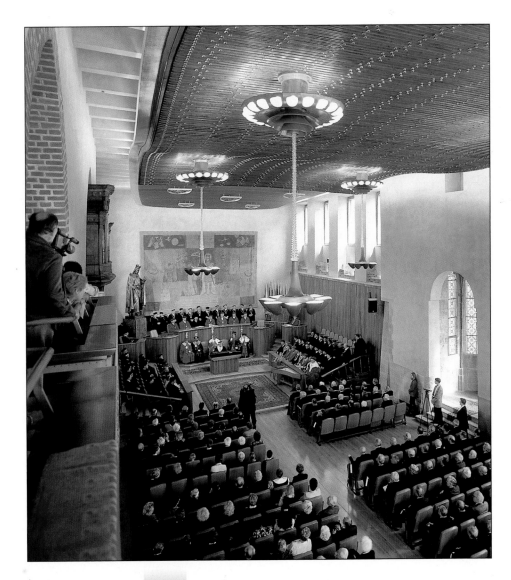

The Estates Theater

The Estates Theater was built in 1781–83 through the benevolence of Franz Anton Nostitz-Rieneck according to a design by Antonín Haffenecker. On 29 October 1787 the theater witnessed the world premiere of the opera *Don Giovanni* by Wolfgang Amadeus Mozart. For the Czech national revival movement, the premises of the theater are associated with the Czech opera *Dráteník* (The Tinker) of 1827 by František Škroup and above all with the comedy *Fidlovačka* (The Spring Fair) by Josef Kajetán Tyl with music by Škroup, in which on 21 December 1834 the song "Kde domov můj" (Where is my homeland?), later the Czech national anthem, was performed for the first time. An important period for the history of the theater was 1813–16, when the opera director here was the composer Karl Maria von Weber. The entrance to the Estates Theater is at Železná Street 540/11

The Church of St. Giles

High above the roofs of this part of the Old Town project the nave and tower of the Church of St. Giles (Jiljí), whose entrance is from Hus Street (Husova ulice). This Gothic church on the site of an original small Romanesque church was ordered built in the fourteenth century by Bishop John IV of Dražice and Archbishop Arnošt of Pardubice. In 1364–74 the preacher Jan Milíč of Kroměříž worked here, and starting in 1420 the priest was Jan of Příbram, a representative of the moderate wing of the Hussites. After the Battle on White Mountain the church was acquired by the Dominican Order, which added a cloister, and in the middle of the eighteenth century the church was remodelled in Baroque style. The church vaults are ornamented by frescos of Václav Vavřinec Reiner, and the plaster decorations are by Bernardo Spinetti. The painting on the main altar, The Founding of the Dominican Order, is by Anthony Stevens

The Church of St. Martin in the Wall

When the fortifications of the Old Town were built in 1240, the Church of St. Martin in the Wall, on Martin Street not far from the Coal Market and Havel Market-place remained partly within and partly outside the ramparts – hence the name "in the Wall". Nearby stood the St. Martin City Gate. The church was remodelled in Gothic style after 1350 and yet again after 1480. It is famous as the place where, already in 1414 at the instigation of Jakoubek of Stříbro, the priest Jan of Hradec served communion in both kinds to the congregation. This significant act was discussed in writing beforehand with Jan Hus, who was imprisoned in Constance at the time. The renovation of the Church at the beginning of the twentieth century was partly the work of the important architect Kamil Hilbert, to whom was entrusted also the completion of St. Vitus Cathedral

The Bethlehem Chapel

This church was erected in 1391–94 thanks to the royal courtier Hanuš of Mühlheim and Councillor Kříž of the Old Town. The chapel is inseparably connected with the work of Jan Hus and Jakoubek of Stříbro. In 1521 the German reformer Thomas Münzer preached here. The church could hold 3,000 people, and besides common people also part of the court of King Wenceslas (Václav) IV came here regularly to hear Jan Hus's preaching, including possibly his wife Žofie, who was among the Hus's supporters. After having been torn down, the church was rebuilt by the Czechoslovak State in the 1950s according to a plan by Josef Fragner. The walls today are decorated with paintings from the Jena Codex, the Richental Chronicle, and the Velislav Bible. Important social and cultural events are held in the chapel, and the hall serves for festive ceremonies of the Czech Technical University (České vysoké učení technické)

The Ungelt

Behind the Church of the Virgin Mary Before Týn on Old Town Square there stood already in the eleventh century a walled princely court serving as a center of international trade, and a customs office where tariffs were collected from foreign merchants bringing goods to Prague. The court also included a hospital, buildings where merchants and their fellow travellers could rest, and horse stables.

The court was called Týn, meaning a demarcated court or space, or also Ungelt, meaning tarriff office. Its original layout of an open space surrounded by buildings with two gates has been preserved to this day. The original Ungelt building was owned in the mid-sixteenth century by Jakub Granovský of Granov, the tariff collector at the time, who had it rebuilt at great expense in Renaissance style. The courtyard

wing of the building has a splendid Renaissance balcony decorated with paintings and sgraffito ornamentation. We can reach the Ungelt from Old Town Square via Týn Lane (Týnská ulička) around the historic building U kamenného zvonu (At the Stone Bell – from the fourteenth century), and if we pass through the east gate from the Ungelt we enter the space in front of St. Jacob's Church, at Malá Štupartská Street 635/6

St. Jacob's Church

Around 1230 King Wenceslas I founded a monastery for the Mendicant Order of St. Francis next to the Romanesque Church of St. Jacob. The Gothic church in its present layout was built during the reigns of Jan Lucemburský and Charles IV. It is not without interest that Jan Lucemburský held his wedding banquet in the monastery here after his marriage to Eliška Přemyslovna. The church acquired its Baroque form during a remodelling in the late seventeenth and early eighteenth centuries, after it burned in 1689. Especially valuable are the stucco decorations on the facade by Ottavio Mosto, capturing scenes from the life of St. Francis, St. Jacob, and St. Anthony of Padua. Today the church is famous above all for its organ and vocal concerts

The Clam-Gallas Palace

On Hus Street (Husova ulice) in the Old Town our attention is drawn to the statues by Matthias Bernhard Braun on the portal to the Clam-Gallas Palace. The diplomat and deputy to the King of Naples Johann Wenzel Gallas had it built at the beginning of the eighteenth century in Baroque style according to a design of the Viennese architect Johann Bernard Fischer von Erlach. The construction was completed by Filip Josef Gallas and modified after 1800 when the owner was Christian Filip Clam-Gallas. Presently the palace houses the Prague City Archive with its old municipal books, etchings, maps, and photographs. Concerts of classical music are also held here. From the Clam-Gallas Palace we may continue on to Marian Square (Mariánské náměstí) with its New Municipal Hall in Art Nouveau style, or set out on Charles Street (Karlova ulice) toward the Charles Bridge (Karlův most)

LILIOVÁ
STARÉ MĚSTO · PRAHA 1

Charles Street and Lily Street

The corner building "U Zlatého hada" (At the Golden Serpent) No. 181/18 stands at the junction of Charles Street (Karlova ulice) and Lily Street (Liliová ulice). This age-old, originally Renaissance building is interesting as the place where, at the beginning of the eighteenth century, coffee was first served. It was brewed by Armén Deodatus Amajan, who lived here and owned the first Prague coffee house, in the building "U Tří pštrosů" (At the Three Ostriches) by the end of the Charles Bridge on the Lesser Side.

We see here the Italian Chapel (Vlašská kaple) and the Church of St. Clement, which today belongs to the Greek Orthodox Church. Folowing around the Church, we come to Knights of the Cross Square (Křižovnické náměstí).

The facade adorned with stucco reliefs of saints – Wenceslas (Václav), Jan Nepomuk, Roch, Sebastian, Ignace of Loyola, Francis Xavier, and Rosalia – by the sculptor J. O. Mayer belongs to the house "U Zlaté studně" (At the Golden Well) at Charles Street No. 175/3. At the center of the decorations is the Virgin Mary with the Divine Infant, surrounded by little angels. This originally Romanesque building acquired its present form during the late Baroque period

The Chapel of Mirrors

T he splendid Chapel of Mirrors is found in a wing of the Clementinum (Klementinum) in the fourth courtyard. It was erected after 1720 by the architect František Maxmilián Kaňka. In the rich plaster decorations of the walls are set mirrors, which give the chapel its name. Its premises are utilized for concerts by chamber music ensembles. The complex of the Clementinum, spread out on the space between Marian Square, Charles Street, Knights of the Cross Square (Křižovnické náměstí), and the streets Křižovnická and Platnéřská, was built starting in the mid-sixteenth century by the Jesuits. After dissolution of the Jesuit Order in 1773, the Clementinum was acquired by the Charles-Ferdinand University. The whole complex boasts precious artistic works. Perhaps the best known is the University Library (today the National Library – Národní knihovna), whose collections include many rare books

Magical Prague

T he view across the towers and
rooftops of churches on Knights of
the Cross Square to the Prague Castle is
truly magical. The Churches of St.

Clement and St. Salvador, which were
part of the Jesuit complex, are complemented by the dome of the Church of
St. Francis of Assisi and the Old Town

Bridge Tower. Knights of the Cross
Square at the end of the Charles Bridge
is often called the smallest and most
beautiful square in Prague

Knights of the Cross Square

Two churches face Knights of the Cross Square (Křižovnické náměstí). The Church of St. Francis of Assisi, associated with the Monastery of the Order of the Knights of the Cross with the Red Star, with its typical dome, was built at the end of the seventeenth century according to a design by Jean-Baptiste Mathey in collaboration with the builder Domenico Giovanni Canevalle. An interesting fresco, The Last Judgment, on the vault of the dome and paintings of the Apostles and Church Fathers – all the work of Václav Vavřinec Reiner – as well as sculptures by Matěj Václav Jäckel and J. A. Quittainer decorate the interior of the church. The Church of St. Salvador, facing the bridge, was founded by the Jesuits at the end of the sixteenth century. Its characteristic pair of towers was modified into its present form in 1714 by František Maxmilián Kaňka. The portico, on which are placed statues of saints by Jan Jiří Bendl, is the work of architect Domenico Galli. On the square stands a Neo-Gothic monument to the Father of the Homeland, Charles IV. It was installed here in honor of the 500th anniversary of the founding of the Charles University

Gallery
of Statues

The view of the Old Town Bridge Tower and the gallery of statues in the open air lining the rail of the bridge on both sides etches itself into one's memory indelibly. The ensemble of thirty statues and statue groups, predominantly Baroque, complemented in the nineteenth century by several Neo-Gothic and Classical works, is completely unique and admired by all visitors to Prague. The oldest statue on the bridge is that of St. Jan Nepomuk, from 1683. Also much admired is Calvary, and the most beautiful is considered to be the statue group of St. Luitgarda by Matthias Bernard Braun. In addition to works by this famous sculptor, statues by M. V. Jäckel, F. M. Brokof, J. O. Mayer, J. B. Kohl, and Josef and Emanuel Max are also set on the bridge

The Rudolfinum

The central hall of the Rudolfinum on Jan Palach Square is the Dvořák Hall, the site of important concerts of the Prague Spring Festival. Since 1945 it has been the home of the Czech Philharmonic, an ensemble raised to world-class quality by its conductors Václav Talich, Rafael Kubelík, Karel Ančerl, and Václav Neumann. The surrounding high row of columns in the musical hall is derived from the interior of the theater in the Palace of Versailles, and the hall is considered to be the most noble Prague interior of the nineteenth century. In viewing the Neo-Renaissance building of the Rudolfinum on the high embankment across the Vltava from the Lesser Side, let us mention that in medieval times this was the outskirts of the Old Town and the Jewish Quarter, as commemorated to this day by the street name "Na Rejdišti" (On the Playground)

The Church of Saints Simon and Jude

This originally Gothic church from the middle of the fourteenth century was rebuilt in the early seventeenth century in Gothic-Renaissance style. A protestant church belonging to the United Brethren, it was assigned after 1620 to the Order of the Brothers of Mercy. The church and its monastery including a hospital were rebuilt in the mid-eighteenth century in Baroque style according to a plan by Jan Jiří Hrdlička. The originally small hospital was expanded to larger proportions, and later further enlarged in the direction of the embankment, so that the whole complex occupies most of the area between the streets U Milosrdných (At the Merciful Brothers) and Na Františku (at St. Francis). In the church is a valuable painting of Simon and Jude by Václav Vavřinec Reiner and on the side altar a painting of St. John of God by Jan Rudolf Bys. Apart from their primary mission, the cloister and hospital have been known for musical activities and are associated with a whole series of musicians, e.g. pupils of Joseph Haydn. The composer František Xaver Brixi died in the hospital here in 1771. Music history recalls also the name of Jan Theobald Held, head of the hospital here and an excellent musician. Today the church has been deconsecrated and serves as a concert hall. Members of Pavel Šmok's Prague ballet ensemble dance here to Antonín Dvořák's Stabat Mater

The Municipal Cultural Hall

The best known Art Nouveau Building in Prague is the Municipal Cultural Hall (Obecní dům), erected as a dignified showplace for the city of Prague in 1905–11. It stands alongside the age-old Powder Tower (Prašná brána), on the site where in medieval times the Royal Court was located. The main facade of the building faces Republic square (náměstí Republiky) and Hybernia Street. Its central portico is adorned with a splendid Art Nouveau entry marquis, and in the rounded gable a mosaic celebrating the city of Prague. Outstanding Czech artists of the time – Alfons Mucha, Ladislav Šaloun, Josef Wenig, Antonín Štrunc, Čeněk Vosmík, Bohumil Kafka, František Ženíšek, Max Švabinský, Josef Pekárek, Karel Novák, Karel Špillar, and others – contributed to decorating the exterior and interior of the Municipal Cultural Hall, whose architects were Osvald Polívka and Antonín Balšánek. The central focal point of the Municipal Cultural Hall is the Smetana Auditorium; worthy of special note is also the Mayor's Salon with decoration by Alfons Mucha

Paris Avenue and Maisel Street

At the end of the nineteenth century the City Council designated for urban renewal (asanace) the whole northern portion of the Old Town, from Old Town Square to the Vltava. A considerable part of this land designated for renewal lay in Josefov, i.e. the former Jewish ghetto. All that survived of it were the synagogues – the Old-New, Klaus, Maisel, Pinkas, High, and on Dušní Street the New Spanish Synagogue – and the historic Old Jewish Cemetery and the Jewish Town Hall. The axis of the section of urban renewal became Asanační Avenue, today Paris Avenue, along which showcase apartment houses of several floors were built, predominantly with Art Nouveau and eclectic facades. The Svatopluk Čech Bridge (Čechův most) in Art Nouveau style, designed by the architect Jan Koula, links to Paris Avenue (Pařížská třída). The originally-planned continuation of the street

through the tunnel in Letná Hill all the way to Bubeneč was not completed. The narrower Maisel Street (Maiselova ulice) runs essentially parallel toward Old Town Square, with similar types of buildings. Both streets today, just as after their construction, are alive with urban and tourist bustle

Art Nouveau Interiors

On Paris, Maisel, Broad (Široká), and Carp (Kaprova) Streets are Art Nouveau buildings erected in 1903–1912 and decorated with typical elements of Art Nouveau interiors. In many buildings we see beautiful windows on staircase landings, original mosaic floors, wainscoting on walls, staircase and elevator grilles with Art Nouveau ornamentation, plaster decoration of ceilings in vestibules, and transoms above doors shaped in Art Nouveau fashion. Among the most effective Art Nouveau decorations of interiors are windows, in which a typically Art Nouveau bird often appears – the peacock

The Old-New Synagogue

One of the most precious historical buildings in Prague is usually considered to be the Old-New Synagogue (Staronová synagoga) at the corner of Červená (Red) and Maisel Streets, from around the year 1270. Evidently the construction team that was finishing the Anežka Cloister at the time shared in its erection. The synagogue is terminated on the east and west sides by high brick gables of the late Gothic type, even though its appearance today is marked by the purist restoration of architect Josef Mocker in 1883. In the interior many Gothic and early Renaissance ornamental elements have been preserved. Especially remarkable is the peaked portal at the entrance from the late thirteenth century with its tympanum, whose surface is decorated with reliefs of grape leaves and grapes. Worship services are held regularly in the Old-New Synagogue. The corner of Červená and Maisel Streets is occupied

by the Jewish Town Hall, capped with a slender tower.

Today's appearance of this building stems from a remodelling after the mid-eighteenth century directed by architect Josef Schlesinger. In 1908 it was expanded to include a wing on Maisel Street. Visitors' attention is drawn above all to the clock with Hebrew numbering

The Old Jewish Cemetery

Today the Old Jewish Cemetery (Starý židovský hřbitov) forms a green oasis of peace in the middle of the city, in the space between the streets U Starého hřbitova (By the Old Cemetery), Břehová (Embankment), 17. listopadu (17 November), and Široká (Broad). On Old Synagogue Street the buildings of the Ceremonial Hall and the Klaus Synagogue rim the cemetery, and on the other side on Broad Street the Pinkas Synagogue. The cemetery was established sometime in the first half of the fifteenth century: the first written report of a cemetery in this location is dated 1440. About 12,000 gravestones are here. The oldest, marking the grave of Avigdor Kara, is from 1439. This sacred place is not omitted in visits to Prague even by important political and cultural figures, for example President of the United States Bill Clinton

The Maisel
Synagogue

At the end of the sixteenth century the Mayor of the Jewish Community, Mordechai Maisel, had a new synagogue erected in Renaissance style by the builders Juda Coref de Herz and Josef Wahl. Over the centuries the synagogue was seriously damaged by fires several times and lost its Renaissance magnificence. Today's Neo-Gothic appearance of the synagogue is the result of two stages of reconstruction in the nineteenth century. Especially the western facade on Maisel Street and the portico with its trio of peaked entryways creates a clear Neo-Gothic effect. However, despite the extensive structural modifications and the conversion of the exterior and interior to Gothic style, the Maisel Synagogue has retained its late Renaissance core. Today the synagogue is part of the Jewish Museum, and unique collections of synagogue objects are exhibited here

The New Town Hall and Church of the Virgin Mary of the Snows

The New Town Hall (Novoměstská radnice) stands on the largest square in Prague – Charles Square (Karlovo náměstí), which originally was called The Livestock Market. The New Town Hall was mentioned for the first time in 1377. During the course of the fifteenth and sixteenth centuries it was rebuilt several times, and its present appearance is the result of remodelling in the early twentieth century, directed by the architects Antonín Wiehl and Kamil Hilbert

The entrance to the Church of the Virgin Mary of the Snows (kostel Panny Marie Sněžné) today is from Jungmann Square (Jungmannovo náměstí). The magnificently conceived structure from the time of Charles IV was never completed in its entirety. Only the chancel, whose vault is the highest in Prague, was completed. At the beginning of the seventeenth century the church was acquired by the Franciscans, who rebuilt and expanded the original Carmellite cloister adjacent to the church.

Both landmarks are closely connected with the dramatic events of Czech history in 1419. The date of 30 July 1419 is often called the beginning of the Hussite Revolution. On this day a large number of advocates of the chalice (i. e. of communion in both kinds) and especially of Jan Želivský, who preached in the unfinished Church of the Virgin Mary of the Snows, assembled here to hear him. After the sermon the Hussites set out with him at their head through the streets of the New Town and at the New Town Hall demanded release of their supporters from imprisonment. The Catholic councilors, however, answered them from the windows of the Town Hall with insults and perhaps with stones, and so the assembled crowd broke into the Town Hall and threw the City Council out of the window onto spears and pitchforks. The leaders of the people, who included Jan Žižka of Trocnov, then established Hussite rule over the New Town

Wenceslas Square

Originally called the Horse Market, this square originated in association with construction of the New Town under the reign of Charles IV. The name Wenceslas Square (Václavské náměstí) has been used since 1848. This square is the main artery of Prague and a center of commercial and cultural life. It is almost a half mile long, and two hundred feet wide. Since the mid-nineteenth century it has gradually changed to an urban boulevard, and in the modern era a new character of architecture has developed, so that the buildings are mostly Neo-Renaissance, Neo-Baroque, and Art Nouveau. Architecture from the most modern periods has been used here as well. The upper part of the square, where the city gate stood, is dominated today by the Neo-Renaissance building of the National Museum. The square has many famous buildings – above all the Art Nouveau Hotel Evropa and the hotels Ambassador and Zlatá husa (The Golden Goose), the Koruna Palace, and the Peterka Building No. 777/12, a noble Art Nouveau structure by architect Jan Kotěra

The National Museum

The monumental Neo-Renaissance building of the National Museum (Národní
muzeum) closes off the upper part of
Wenceslas Square. It was erected in
1885–1890 according to a design by Josef
Schulz. The sculptural decoration of the
facade is by Antonín Wagner, Josef Mauder,
Antonín Popp, Bohuslav Schnirch, František
Hergesel, Antonín Procházka, Josef

Strachovský, and others. Below the museum is an equestrian monument to St.
Wenceslas (sv. Václav) from 1912 by Josef
Václav Myslbek. Prince Wenceslas is surrounded by statues of Czech saints –
Prokop, Vojtěch (Adalbert), Ludmila, and
Anežka (Agnes). Alois Dryák shared in
designing the monument, and the ornamentation is the work of Prof. Celda Klouček

The National Museum, Interior

The showplace of the National Museum is the Pantheon, where important social and cultural events are held. It is dedicated to the memory of figures important in Czech history, whose busts and bronze statues adorn the whole space. The wall murals were painted by František Ženíšek and Václav Brožík. The Pantheon occupies all floors of the front tract and has a glass dome. The decorative paintings beneath it are the work of Vojtěch Hynais. The Museum Staircase, also decorated with statues and paintings, is a frequent site for concerts organized here "on the stairs". In the National Museum are deposited and exhibited valuable prehistoric, archeological, mineralogical, geological, and zoological collections. The Museum Library contains many precious volumes

The State Opera

Near the Main Train Station (Hlavní nádraží) in Prague stands the Neo-Renaissance building of the State Opera, which was erected according to plans by the Viennese architects Hermann Helmer and Ferdinand Fellner in 1886–87. The building served the New German Theater in Prague, which had a share in introducing the music of Richard Strauss and Gustav Mahler to Bohemia. The theater orchestra maintained direct contacts with Mahler, which significantly contributed to the formation of a Mahler cult in Prague.

On the facade of the theater are busts by the sculptor Otto Menzel, and the gable is adorned by Dionysus and Thalia in chariots – the work of Theodor Friedl

The National Theater

In its stylistic perfection, its architectural beauty, its setting, and its well-thought-out execution, the National Theater (Národní divadlo) represents one of the pinnacles of Czech architecture in the nineteenth century. This building, erected in 1868–83, is associated with the names of architects Josef Zítek and

Josef Schulz, and with a whole series of Czech artists who shared in decorating the exterior and interior. Outstanding decoration is found not only in the theater's foyer but in the hallways leading to the main viewing area and the loges. The stage curtain is the work of painter Vojtěch Hynais, who conceived the painting such as to

celebrate the construction of the National Theater. It captures the artists, workers, and all who shared in the construction along with many particular period details. Above the curtain in the proscenium is expressed the idea of the theater, which originated through nationwide donations – "From the Nation to Itself" (Národ sobě)

Žofín

Already in 1837 there stood on Slavic Island (Slovanský ostrov), earlier called Žofín, a building that became the site of important events in Czech social and political life. The building acquired its present form through reconstruction and expansion in 1886. The original name of the island, Žofín, was adopted as the name of the structure. With Žofín, which is in the immediate vicinity of the National Theater, is associated a tradition of great concerts and Czech balls. Among others Franz Liszt and Hector Berlioz concertized here. The patterned ceiling of the great hall of Žofín was painted by František Duchoslav and the four figures are the work of Viktor Oliva. Žofín is alive with social events still today

Masaryk Embankment

One of the most pleasant and beautiful walks through the center of Prague is along the Masaryk Embankment and on along the Rašín Embankment (Masarykovo nábřeží) to Vyšehrad. Especially in the segment between the National Theater and Jirásek Square we can observe a broken, wavy wall of imposing buildings of several stories with facades in imitation of historical styles and in the Art Nouveau style of the early twentieth century. Gables and turrets of the most varied shapes, balconies, architectural sculpture, stucco ornamentation on plant or animal motives, and paintings on the facades capture our attention. Building No. 236/30 from 1905, built by Jan Brzák, may serve as an example: its facade is adorned with paintings capturing scenes from the construction of the embankment here

Masaryk Embankment Interiors

The interiors of the vast majority of buildings on the Masaryk Embankment are magnificently executed with dignified vestibules, broad staircases, and decoration sometimes to the point of pomposity. Glass in the doors and especially the windows utilize the effect of striking color, and with subjects using predominantly the Art Nouveau motives of the peacock, landscapes, or flower patterns, the etched glass creates an impression of delicacy. Staircase railings are formed into flowered or geometrical patterns, and the doors in the interiors have etched Art Nouveau arches and are decorated with transoms above. The interiors of Neo-Gothic buildings imitate the reception halls of late Gothic bourgeois homes. The result attests to the great erudition of designers of the time and the skill of craftsmen

Hlahol

Building No. 238/16 from 1905 was erected according to plans of Josef Fanta for the patriotic singing society Hlahol (meaning "clamor"). Karel Mottl and Josef Pekárek worked with the architect on the decoration. The dominant element of the facade is a massive, segmented gable, whose space is filled with a colored ceramic mosaic picture with symbols of song and music. Even a ceramic picture of the mythical peacock is on hand, around the entrance to the building. The nobility of the hall in the building consists mainly in a painting by Alfons Mucha from 1921 called Song. Bronze plaques on the facade commemorate three important chorus masters of Hlahol – Karel Bendl, Karel Knittl, and Bedřich Smetana

The Dancing Building

On the site of a building that was bombed in 1945 arose in 1992–96 the "Dancing Building" by architects Frank O. Gehry and Vlado Milunić, and formed a special, completely modern corner of Jirásek Square and the Rašín Embankment. The bold exterior of the building as a whole does not disturb the appearance of the row along the embankment, which represents architecture of the early twentieth century. Next to the Dancing Building is the Art Nouveau building "U Dvou tisíc" (At Two Thousand), No. 2000/78, which Václav Havel (grandfather of the modern president) had built in 1904

Buildings
Beneath Vyšehrad

The buildings beneath Vyšehrad ("The Castle on the Height") show very interesting architecture from the late nineteenth and early twentieth centuries. For example, in Vratislav Street there is a whole row of Neo-Renaissance buildings whose facades, today mostly renovated, attest to the taste and wealth of those who built them. The building called "U Kroka" (Krok's House), No. 28/12 on Vratislav Street, was built in 1896 according to a plan by Josef Filipovský. The decoration of the facade is highlighted by pendants of fruit and half columns with Ionic caps; areas of exposed brick masonry alternate with stucco. The name of the building is clearly supported by a fine portrait of Prince Krok. The adjacent building No. 29/10 from 1910 was erected also in a Neo-Renaissance style, by František Josef Hodek. On the interesting arched gable the sgrafito decoration with plant motives and portraits is outstanding

Cubism Below Vyšehrad

From the Imperial Meadow (Císařská louka), an island beneath Vyšehrad with access from Smíchov on the opposite bank, there are fine views of the Vyšehrad cliff with its medieval fortifications, the Church of Saints Peter and Paul, and the cubist buildings and villas on the embankment below the cliff. Here on the Imperial Meadow, earlier called the Chapter Island, we are also aware of the strategic position of this second Prague castle, which guarded the approach to the city from this side and via the river. At the beginning of the twentieth century a tunnel was dug through the Vyšehrad cliff, resulting in direct connection of the city with the suburban sections beyond the cliff

In few places in Prague do we find so many architectural reminders of the relatively short period of cubism as beneath Vyšehrad. On the corner of Neklan and Přemysl Streets stands a building at No. 98 with a cubist facade by Josef Chochol, built in 1913–14. The sharp corner supports the balcony of the five-angle layout. The building is one of the foremost examples of Czech cubist architecture. Additional cubist buildings may be found in Vnislav and Libuše Streets and on the embankment beneath the Vyšehrad cliff

The Gates to Vyšehrad

The medieval gates to Vyšehrad have not survived with the exception of a torso of the south gate, called Point (Špička) because of the large number of pyramidal roofs. We find the torso of Špička halfway between the gates shown in the pictures. The southernmost, late Renaissance gate in the Vyšehrad fortifications, called the Tábor Gate, was built in the 1640s. The second gate, in Baroque style – the Leopold Gate – was completed in the 1670s. It has a very interesting facade ornamented with sculpture. Its construction was begun by the architect Carlo Lurago and completed by the Giovani Decapauli. To the Leopold Gate are joined Baroque brick ramparts built according to a plan by Count Inocenc Conti

St. Martin's Rotunda
The Vyšehrad Park

E vidently sometime around the year 1100, in the area within the outer medieval fortifications of Vyšehrad, close to the road passing through them, was built the Rotunda of St. Martin. In the Middle Ages this chapel served choir members of the Vyšehrad Chapter Church. In the seventeenth century it was a storehouse for gun powder for the Vyšehrad fortress. In the second half of the nineteenth century the crumbling rotunda was rented to the poor for housing. Not until the end of the nineteenth century was the chapel returned to its original mission. We catch sight of St. Martin's Rotunda immediately after passing through the Leopold Gate, on the right along the route we may take for a walk through the fortress, enjoying the views of the city

O n the lawn where once stood the palace of the Czech princes and the Gothic castle of Charles IV are found today four statue groups by Josef Václav Myslbek. These enormous works, on motives from Czech myths, stood by the Palacký Bridge until 1947. The Chapter and Parish Church of Saints Peter and Paul acquired its present form when its Gothic style was renewed by architects Josef Mocker and František Mikš at the end of the nineteenth century and beginning of the twentieth. On the other side of the Vyšehrad church lies the cemetery with its Slavín (Pantheon). We can also visit the museum, the church, and the underground passages. The park treatment of Vyšehrad offers the visitor rest, and a circle walk along the ramparts with views on the city and the river is a unique experience

The Church of Saints Peter and Paul

The interior of the Church of Saints Peter and Paul at Vyšehrad attracts the visitor's attention first of all with its Art Nouveau figural and ornamental decoration, created by the married couple František and Marie Urban in 1902–03. They were also responsible for the lunettes in the loft on both sides of the nave, for which they used motives from the beginnings of Christianity in the Czech lands and from the history of Vyšehrad during the reign of King Vratislav. The Altar of the Czech Patrons, an Art Nouveau work by Jan Kastner from 1910, harmonizes well with the paintings. A Romanesque sarcophagus from the eleventh to twelfth centuries, called the Tomb of St. Longin, reminds us of early Vyšehrad. However, the furnishings of the church are predominantly Neo-Gothic

Painting of the Virgin Mary of the Rain

T he miraculous painting of the Virgin Mary of the Rain (Panna Marie Dešťová), found in the third chapel of the Vyšehrad church on the right, is an outstanding example of Czech Gothic painting from the mid-fourteenth century. The painting comes from the collections of Emperor Rudolf II and was donated to the Vyšehrad church by Rudolf's secretary Ondřej Hannevald of Eckersdorf. Processions came to this painting to pray for rain and according to an old legend it was painted by the hand of St. Luke

The Vyšehrad Cemetery

T he most often visited place at Vyšehrad is the cemetery, whose central focal point is the Slavín (Pantheon) – a common tombstone for important figures in Czech social and cultural history. The architectural treatment of the Slavín and the cemetery arcades was designed by Antonín Barvitius and Antonín Wiehl, who impressed a Neo-Renaissance quality on the whole complex. An important role in the sepulchral treatment was played by artists of the Art Nouveau period. The tombstone with the bust of the composer Antonín Dvořák was created by sculptor Ladislav Šaloun. A representative of Czech symbolism, František Bílek produced the symbolistic statue Žal (Woe) on the grave of the writer Václav Beneš Třebízský

Vyšehrad Legends

F ew places are so woven with myths and legends as the age-old Vyšehrad, forever associated with the mythical mother Libuše from the princely Přemysl family. Princess Libuše foretold the glory of Prague and the Czech nation, but also its suffering. Beneath the Vyšehrad cliff the river allegedly hides the treasure of Princess Libuše. According to legend Libuše had her baths where now lie the remnants of the ramparts on the cliff, which we know are a torso of the medieval guard station. The magic of Vyšehrad and its sacred atmosphere of special peace affects perhaps every receptive visitor.

Since time immemorial the Vyšehrad cliff with its castle formed the gateway to Prague from the south, while on the other side the city was guarded by the Prague Castle

AN ILLUSTRATED GUIDE TO
PRAGUE

Photographs by Jiří Všetečka
Cover design and graphics by Václav Rytina
Translation into English David R. Beveridge
First edition, Prague, 1998
Issued by V RÁJI Publishers
(Prague-1, Maiselova Street 12/76, Czech Republic),
as its 84th publication, 148 pages, 170 color photographs
Responsible editors Marie Vitochová and Jindřich Kejř
Printed by Východočeská tiskárna, s. r. o.
(East Bohemia Printers, limited), Pardubice, Czech Republic